Burning the Heartwood

Also by Janet Sutherland:

Crossing Over

JANET SUTHERLAND

BURNING THE HEARTWOOD

Shearsman Books
Exeter

Published in the United Kingdom in 2006 by
Shearsman Books Ltd
58 Velwell Road
Exeter EX4 4LD

ISBN-10 0-907562-88-4

ISBN-13 978-0-907562-88-7

Acknowledgements
Some of the poems collected here have previously appeared, or
will appear, in *Angels of Fire, Damn the Caesars, Kudos, Litter, Ninth
Decade, Poesie Europe, Shearsman, Sow's Ear, Stride, The News, The
Rialto*, as well as in the following anthologies: *Angels of Fire.
An Anthology of Radical Poetry in the 80's* (ed. Sylvia Paskin, Jay
Ramsay and Jeremy Silver, Chatto and Windus, 1986); *Dancing
the Tightrope. New Love Poems by Women* (ed. Barbara Burford,
Lindsay MacRae & Sylvia Paskin, 1987); *The New British Poetry
1968-88* (ed. Gillian Allnutt, Fred D'Aguiar, Ken Edwards, Eric
Mottram, Paladin Poetry, 1988); *Reality Studios, Vol 6: Interface*
(ed. Ken Edwards, 1984); *The Virago Book of Love Poetry* (ed.
Wendy Mulford, 1990). Thanks to all the editors and publishers
for their support.

The publisher gratefully acknowledges financial assistance from
Arts Council England.

CONTENTS

For Lesley and Joseph

Hearth

The hiss of flame before earth

Sometimes the ear listens
without thought

Unbuttoning the heart
we hear rain
from a wet coat
leaping and cracking
on stone

During long walks

During long walks
a small stone placed in one shoe
anchors the thoughts

Fragment 31

Opposite you he sits,
this man, equal with the gods,
listening to you –
your sweet speech

and your laughter. My heart
lurches when I look
at you, even briefly.
I cannot speak.

My tongue is stopped.
A sly flame runs
under my skin. I can
see nothing. My ears hum.

Sweat drenches me.
I tremble, bleached like
grass. I have come
closer, now, to death.

Cinnabar

He gave me cinnabar, in a small suitcase,
just before my ship sailed out of port.
In the first days when I dare not walk
on deck I would look at the red stain
on the soiled leather and remember his
hands. Each morning I checked the old
barometer for weather, *heel schoon*
it said and the sea was flat, silvered.
Progress was slow. Sailors called to me.
The captain looked away and would not speak.

Later, a swelling sea, *veranderlyk*, and a coastline
near enough to hear the breakers crashing
against rock. Birds on the cliff tops rising
and wheeling, falling as one, gone to nothing.
Sunsets were vermilion, madder lake.
The water, lapis lazuli and azurite. I could
not sleep. The stars reminded me of home.
A dress hung in my cabin waiting for landfall.
Lamplight drew a face upon its folds.
In the creaking of the timbers I heard voices.

One bone black night, I walked on deck,
a lead white moon dipped in and out. The sea
became the folded downs, a lighthouse flashing
endlessly. Near dawn there came a glimmer
on the waves, a glaze like mercury on glass.
Bestendig then, I took my suitcase out
and opened it, a fine red dust rose up
to darken on the surface of the sea.
Though I am emptied too, my alchemist
spent all the hidden gold he left in me.

Touching heartsease

my little pretty patch of wilderness
hung in the short term
between desire and passion
turgid with flowers –
broad iris buds
drift of forget
me nots
mazy with sleep
drawn deep across rain
falling soft
warm silent
in a deepening green

today no edges are visible
colour melts back
this is a veiny petal
place
warm laved under tree
before sun
wet with translucence

we wait here without memory
swimming and drowning
touching heartsease
and approaching
honesty

Another poem

those hands that plunge
loam caked to plant
and fish for white roots
in a lusty soil

have rummaged among maps
to find a route through
wrinkled terraces
indented coombes

you wait to find the sun
to touch
the folded valleys
with a careful thumb

summits and ridges
bound in miniature
your contours plotted
on the edge of spring

Cirrus in bed

I would put
cirrus or
cirrocumulus
to bed
to lay a hair-like filament
across your face

high up a banded linear event
perplexes thought
but wrapped in lace
you open up to touch it with your tongue

In the green and gold of the light

the woman under the tree is
showered with flowers falling
from above
they are paper purple hearts
in the field beyond lie crowns
abundant   i enter your dream
quietly and later find myself
tilling the earth

Seed

we are making a path
collecting stones
flint and old buttons from a dead mans shirt

I have let seed fall
here, the tares and the foxgloves drift in
under cover of darkness

birds shit pips into the cracks, the thorns
of the blackberry
harden, tough

skinned stone breaks
and the buds open

Agnes

Agnes has planted her onions
in good time – thin green shoots rise
in rows. She works her shallow hoe
through rampant weeds in May.
In summer buttressed ranks seed blue
and blowsy globes. Still air
surrounds the pungent humid depths
where ants and woodlice journey
over cracking soil. The swelling domes,
the paper-covered monuments
she harvests slowly against winter.
The seasons fit seamlessly one against
the other; her sorrows have many layers.

The stringing of onions

I pushed them in the soil
and left them to grow

on midwinter nights
frost crackled the touch-papers

green tapers pierced spring
each one alone

rising. Minarets, a sky of them
silent, the hidden blue

waiting. On hot still days
tough hollow stems

buttressed the seed-heads
for snails with small intricate shells

to rest on.

Firework

Touch paper
and stand back

ushering kids beyond
the imaginary line
and handing out sparklers

had i forgotten
the fire coming out
as crystals of ice

staring at the diminishing line
tracing a name in joined-up writing
before

Revisions

She woke considering the evidence:
the brown dog was still howling
in the frozen yard. Since suppertime
the stubble field, its bedded flint
and cold dark loam, had shrunk.
The wisp of snipe had gone
along with the fall of woodcock.
A cup of water by the bed
was porcelain not solid earthenware
and Spring had receded. It was snowing again.

The punctuation of her thought had changed
as had its metaphor. Field water
in thin, clouded sheets hung cold
across depressions in the rutted land,
and now the hill was not personified
she missed its female curve, the tender slope
that led to knotted copses, undergrowth,
and places she could visit on her own.
The dog was brown, her cup was porcelain,
her thought as delicate as ice.

Resented but adored, the howling dog
would be replaced. She loved the sag
of skin around his jaw, the piebald gum,
the touch of tartar on his canine teeth,
the rough feel of coarse hair along his shoulder
blades. But when his constant voice had gone
what alteration would she find to yard,
to house, and to herself who sheltered there
because the dog loved her? She woke
considering the evidence.

Blackbirds flying

white threadbare linen, hooks removed,
steeped, pounded, placed in vats
and raised in mesh to drain
then dry,
compressed

a winter sub-song heard from undergrowth

as iron gall, dark like a black bird's eye
flowed from the sharpened quill, gum
arabic prevented feathering

the warning call with flicking wings and tail

sometimes the sonnet put itself aside
for lists of births and deaths and marriages,
the cost of fish and ale and wheat for baking bread

a loud and pleasing warbling flutelike song

a cadence rising delicate might be
a broken arc of shell in greenish blue
another place to move to outside this

on the edges of dense woodland, a song post
as permanent as paper scratched with ink

Itching

mostly I was itching
to be out, putting tubers
in the ground, waiting
for mystery to come
wriggling in slow time
between grains of sand

I was hearing the crackle
of water easing through
membranes, the wet slop
in cells un-starched after winter
I was putting soil so deep
in the creases of my hand

seed grew there. Roots
writhed through channels —
blood, bone. Intricately
circled the twinned
hemispheres following
folds, convoluted, strange.

words were unmade
there, parted, detached
sucked salty and strong
up all the branching paths
a rough stream singing
many different songs

Memory

the little adders fall
out of the pitch-forked hay

into the stooks
floating the swollen river

the past like folded washing
dislocates

the last bus missed
the fifteen mile walk home

a carthorse ridden standing
to a quiet stall

speaking in fragments
still

the lost and agile words
could be a poem

an adder falling
punctuates the peace

an image of skin . . .

an image of skin I once knew intimately
like water stalled below a bank of autumn trees

mirrored; unreachable as trout,
slipping under an eel trap for shelter

in the dust under the willows
the heifers stand idly

dung-laden tails swish
to their round swollen bellies,

some of them swam to the bull
on the other side, risking the current

and had to be fetched home
long miles in a lorry

and I count them, their little bastards
growing unplanned

like water stalled below a bank of autumn trees
mirrored, unreachable as trout

Cat got your tongue?

Cat got your tongue?
they'd say
and mother would help
dishing out words
with comfortable ease
not quite but near enough

now the mind falters
seeing your lips
smiling mouthing
the phrase that is less
than not quite

'picture' was the object
so 'it hangs on a wall
and you look at it
it has a frame and it
imagines something that is
not quite'

but more than
this is the shy tongue
talking by parable(?)
we look at each other
piling up names
reaching past
i would kiss you.

Gossip

as if
sensual pleasure were enough
raw silk at the fingertips
flicker of green and blue in the salt flame

"he said, and she said
in the school yard
with a knot of fisted faces
hanging on each word"

glowing they move in half light
unsolid at the edge
shimmering

In the hospital grounds

In the hospital grounds
the newly blind
learn braille
one of the young trees
has not yet learned compassion
and tells lies

The walled garden

and is this a dream or a torment?

she seems to awake from a trance
and is here in this garden
there is a lawn and she thinks
it is chamomile
the crushed scent is warm
in the air and flowers
move in the borders
sea-like against the weight
of green

she sees that the sky is blue
the sun warm on her head
and listens to the space
between birdsong

the gate to the garden is shut
someone has left her here
in the centre of eden
and she is a statue of stone
yet thinking and feeling

and here is the baby
playing at her feet
and there is the pool
with a bright ball
nestling at its edge

The road to the beach

On the road to the beach
two women and two children
packed in an old van
with two bikes and
assorted clothes for dressing up

the sea is always no further than the bend ahead
and the voice of the youngest singing a travelling song

ascending the cliff steps we talk of other days
your calm voice strengthens in a time of need
solid you rest me in a pool of words
and save me drowning

we have invented wise escapes from quicksand
leaping from the surreal to the ridiculous
and into laughter and agreement

the beach shifts as we walk
on the palm of its hand
(indents in our presence)
head heart and life lines exposed by the tide
i do not think our names will be erased
we scratched them deep and did not watch
the waves come in

the sea is always no further than a down bent head
and the breath of the youngest quieted in sleep

To Patricia (Paddy)

in all this is the courage
you will not sing
mouthing the words at weddings and funerals
in dim churches

once with the sound of the tractor
in the fields you opened your mouth
and let rip
till you knew the low drone of the engine
still let the song out into the open field

with what courage you stumble and fall
work in the cowsheds   dip cold hands in hot water
milk knit garden   moving around the house
in a dance with the sound of the song pouring
around and inside you stopping just short of your mouth
in your mind you sing defiantly
making light
of your body

Speech

He sings and plays the piano
and leaves the French windows open
so that the sound finds me here
glad hearted at the missed notes
and open vowels of the forgotten words
Each night there is more of the song
embellishments are added and trip
over themselves
slow blues melodies of the mission
the warm burr of the voice rising
falling

here in the city the night settles around itself
a last whistled tune and a snatch of song
and after midnight he too
sleeps

the sound of the leaves in high branches
cushions the silence

the small gap of loss
after speech.

An orchard subject 1946

This war time gardener
lauds his sweet cherries:
red turk, ursula rivers, smoky dunn
governor wood, hooker's black and elton heart.

Precisely accurate and dry his text explains
the cuts and mazzard stocks, the tips and tricks
for heavy crops. He mourns the fruits
devoured by birds at cherry picking time.

His sour cherries need no special care;
a passable dessert, he will allow,
when fully ripe. Self fertile, un-acclaimed,
anonymous and humble, fruit for pies —

he sends his female pickers out in pairs
to cut these modest crops. Their constant chat,
an irritant to him and to the birds,
is sweetened, useful, scattered under trees

... unheard, these women mutter constantly,
between the careful lines in counterpoint,
and spit, like restless saboteurs,
delicious, dangerous and tender juice.

Fruit Growing Outdoors — Raymond Bush 1946

The colour of gull's eggs

I could spin them on my table
blur specks to lines

I have eaten gull's eggs
for breakfast. Broken
the olive green, brown-speckled shell
and gorged. Good eating, strong. I strut
along the promenade

I have taken to watching breakwaters
with more than a taste for the architectural
I would like to perch there
in a line with other gulls
watching the tide turn
lifting easily
when the slow swell
swallows the post

I steal
ice cream from toddlers
laughing.
Their empty cones
held high, I am liberty,
outstretched, I bathe in light

From here I can see
what I need. My voice wails, mews,
recedes in a series of diminishing cries.
I have broken the olive green, brown-speckled shell
to strut along the promenade

The Reckless Sleeper (René Magritte)

I keep their relics
close at hand
sometimes the candle flickers
or the bird preens
under my hat
there used to be a pentangle
but I cut it and covered it over
with mercury, it quickens my dreams.
I tasted her apple afterwards,
one bite, and retied her bow.
I make my plans slowly
under this thin blanket
her half of the pillow dented
and the carved curve of her back
as cold as her mirror.

When he had cut up her clothes

When he had cut up her clothes
And burned them
He opened the door
And seeing the cot in the corner
He picked up the baby
And wrapped it in her long red scarf

Dissociation

his finger
dropped off
on the train

it looked like
a small black pudding
with a tiny nail

none of the others
would fall off   everyone
seemed very sure of that

but still
as he ran down the corridor
he kept holding it

and a pink plastic ring
he had bought on holiday

From the street

there's this little girl
four at the outside
standing right there in the window display
rearranging the plastic strawberries
and testing them with her teeth
she hasn't checked to see if the store detective's looking
and she hasn't noticed us admiring her
gall

she has a red dress on
and she's eating strawberries
in her own time

In the house of the terracotta warriors

She walks this house at night
a barren concubine
walled up alone. Her emperor,
who left her here,
has disinterred himself
and gone. She waits for dawn,
the chink of bottles
the receding steps

her stairs are ranked with terracotta warriors
a bleached out infantry
of milk, curdled and sour,
each day brings new recruits
who turn their faces
outwards to the door
a makeshift offering
in this twilight mausoleum
not combat ready,
all unarmed

they speak to her in one
collected voice, mostly commands.
Sometimes she wears
her brothers clothes
for silence. Other days
she puts her red dress on
sits in amongst them,
on the crowded stairs,
singing their anthems
and their battle hymns.

An incident in Vienna (1991)

On my way to the police station
to register as an alien
something fell out of the sky
and hit me on the shoulder

I did not know it was a shoe
at first, having no reason to suspect
a shoe would fall out of the sky,
my first hour in Vienna

What did I do then?
I walked to the body
of the fallen man, the suicide.
Uncertain what to do

I replaced the shoe on his left foot,
the shoeless foot, and looked
at all his spilling pearls, a scattering
of lucid brain and alabaster broken teeth

To the Spider in the crevice
/ behind the toilet door

i have left you four flies
three are in the freezer next to the joint of beef
the other is wrapped in christmas paper
tied with a pink ribbon
beside the ironing table in the hall
should you need to contact me
in an emergency
the number's in the book
by the telephone.

p.s. i love you

Leaning over

Leaning over
to press a little row of
judas kisses
down the length of the spine
he smiles
and tries to remember
her name.

I was quietly writing your name

I was quietly writing your name
In my bowl of porridge
Then pressing the curve of the spoon
Against it, like a lover
Or an eraser

Variegation I

By late evening she was cleaning the sink . . .

off-white at the periphery
— the character of Ivy
depends on a smooth edge

using bleach on the tea stains
carefully, to avoid splashing her hands

on newer stems
this portion of the leaf
is cream
gradually fading with age

she poured a generous measure
down the plughole

variegation is effected
by the grouping together
of different pigments
— light green/dark green,
in some cases
red or other exotic colours

wiping the brass fitting round it
til it shone

two shades of green, quite distinct
and separate,
the darker laid over the fairer

remembering Jim and the young girl
fucking on the spare bed

older leaves lose clarity, gain depth:
greygreen, they are trees in a landscape
further away than you thought

she sees him in the mirror over
the sink and says without
turning —
can i trust you?

Variegation II

Oh, yes . . . as far as the variegated ivy is concerned, I have identified four basic colours of the leaves.

No, sorry, five — of course there are variations, gradations from one to another, but that's a little too sophisticated for the time being — we'll cover that later, if there's time.

colour one, off white, as you can see, found mainly on older leaves at the periphery as if it was necessary for this part of the leaf because if the leaf ceased where the green pigments stopped the line of the edge would be jagged, the character of ivy depends on a smooth edge.

colour two: ditto as for off white, except on new leaves this portion of the leaf is cream.

colour three: light green.

colour four: darker green.

O for a language more colour specific. Light green, dark green what does this specify? For a language with more smells than acrid and pungent. They say instead 'You should have been there, it was good, it was very good' and you should have been there, but if I know you your pleasure in the smoke and fire dimmed by not being able to tell more than a fraction of it, and that fraction, approximate and diffuse and the two greens of the ivy distinct and separate the darker laid over the fairer like lovers lost in the act of love

colour five: greygreen, the older leaves lose clarity, gain depth, the almost blue tinge to trees in a landscape further away than you thought. You see, you can hold middle distance in your hands, and it's a fine thing but fragile, very fragile. Can I trust you? After a while you can be there without trying

Variegation III

The Syrian, tells me a story,
it goes something like this:
a man went to heaven to visit his father
who had died
he had petitioned god who had given him
a visitor's permit
so he could make sure his father was well
and happy
an angel led him to the place where his father was
and left them together
they spoke a while then the man said
who is this beautiful woman who sits so close
beside you
is she your reward?
No, the old man answered,
I am her punishment . . .

a rose creeps among dunes

how a hurled stone
turns in the air

suckering   like a snake

flint points and re-points

in soft sand

it is an arc
over or underarm

thorns tight to the bud

seawards/
purple

a place in
and through
time

mostly unnoticed

Impunity

larks, quails and thrushes
can eat hemlock
with impunity;
a quick breath
and a hasty heart
make their own
approach to a
conclusion

I have slowed my heart
hoping something new
might come
an understanding
of all the arcs —
the slow stones turning
under the sun

What the Keeper saw

trees like ragged lace
along the horizon

woad, weld and madder
fused, workmanlike

and brittle as lichen
knapped flint dark

on unclothed
creamy downs

ten crows on strings
along the holly bough

and bagged across his back
four stoats. He feels their

curious breath, the gift
of ermine in the long dark days

Freedom 1

if, in a once plentiful land,
a small, dry seed
fell onto dusty earth

would you,
like a fleet winged bird,
fly off for water
or swoop down
for a quick feed?

Freedom 2

we have watched
them walk into the wind
and hang in the creak and rustle
of full sails
in the clear air above Mount Caburn

there the words
are the curves of the hill
her creases and shadowed folds
the trickles of scent, fox sharp
among nettles and briars
small furtive movements
and a hawk so high up
silent
still

here the words are
the field boundaries
easing out
the gnarled trees
set in their ways
they are broken and unbroken
promises
taking off,
startled,
thrilled
at the parting

Freedom 3

Trapped like a sepia print
I cannot look you squarely in the eye
You must hold still

Your mind travels
Without permission
To many strange places

Buffalo and wild green maps
Come to your room
An unfriendly chicken

Settles itself on your bed
You pluck at the covers
Sometimes we wave it away

And sometimes we cry
All of us and laugh
Because we are falling

Slowly into another place.
The sampler made in 1824
Reminds us of industry

And improvement
In the young.
Stories weave in and out

Of us.
Then we are still.

Keash Hill

used so to silence
or the murmur of old men
retouching tales of the dead
'the lord have mercy on him'

the green hills
and the grey hills
and the horizon

you want to tell me how it is
to be here
too weak for the mountain
speaking the names of the dead
fleshing their bones

but i found you up here anyway
where the wind blows so strong
it still enters the lungs
like a friend
and speech
buffets at a truth
self evident

If you kiss a mermaid

when you find one high and dry
flies will be sipping at her lips

sand in her gritted eyes
her iridescent scales will bleach

grey down her leaden flank
the silvered fin she spread to swim

will be faded, ragged, rank
beached too far up

among the whitening bones of cuttlefish
the round green eyes of pebbles worn from glass

the odd detritus of a foreign land
surrounding her, an out flung hand

will seem to beckon — don't be taken in
storm tossed, she's just leviathan

in miniature; abandoned, lost
and dying slowly like the rest of us

She sweeps (AD1264 Malling Down, Lewes)

after the battle they caught him
he had tried to run away

the hill above town
was not for common criminals.

they tied his hands
leather measured his pulse

many people stood as witnesses
in silence   skylarks sang

they'd beaten him
his gaze on other earth

gathered his mother to the byre;
an ordinary task

Original

"whilst this planet has gone cycling on according to the fixed law of gravity, from so simple a beginning endless forms most beautiful and most wonderful have been, and are being, evolved."
Charles Darwin, *Origin of Species*, 1859

From so simple a beginning
Endless forms
Most beautiful
Spin out —

That original spare
Curve, the cradling
Of oily eggs
In fetid air

They glimmer
Housed in mud
Invisible from here
But lineal

Like us;
Famine and death
Surround us
We march on

Halcyon days

"It is a Vulgar persuasion, that this bird, being hung up on an untwisted thread by the bill in any room, will turn its Breast to that quarter of the Heaven whence the wind blows: They that doubt of it may try it."

Willoughby, *Ornithology* (1678)

if a single King-fisher
be hanged up
with untwisted silk
where the air is quiet
and unmoved
or, in capacious bell-jars
closely stopped,
a pair be dangled
for experiment:
we'll know which way
the wind blows

Roma

drift of rich voices, scooters, horns
the simple bell of a church sounds the half hour
up on the balcony a light breeze
rustles the flowers, shadows flick
on grey louvered shutters and
a fern swims green
in the space between door and
door   in the solid light
a pomegranate tree fruits out of terracotta
and the long cream flower of thorn apple
holds itself in an instant of perfection
at ground level a harsh glare strikes back
from the clay coloured buildings
but above it's a green city
and with the evening softenings
swallows glide and cry
through the patterning leaves
at our level
and just beyond reach.

Gaps

how that first city began
an act of chance

four trees in a square
with branches interlocked
dry underneath

and you came there
and saw that it might be good
and cut down some of the closest trees
and your friends came
and used the timber to make houses
felled more of the forest to make fields
multiplied in the goodness of the land

how you dug clay to make bricks
coal for fire
precious metals for tools to make intricate playthings

how you settled in hamlets villages towns
and called the gaps country

how you make and destroy and remold
classify name and re-order
leaving nothing untouched
by your constantly restless fingers
and your semi opposable thumbs.

The view

'... And he overthrew those cities, and
all the plain, and all the inhabitants of
the cities, and that which grew upon
the ground. But his wife looked back
from behind him, and she became a
pillar of salt . . .'

Genesis 19 25-26

Unlike Lot's wife she
turned back

not stone, cold bleached
nor man's mate – nameless
woman
not for curiosity
nor pity

not for

at the flash
the balls of her eyes melted

Spider's web

she spins like no other woman
ready or not she is coming

does she have thread?
enough to hang you all
by the coat tails wigs and whiskers
fast and safe

she is swaying gently
forward and back
making patterns of her thoughts

extending
ex tending
she throws out
more than
it
was

can i come close?
yes   if you are she
you are already part of her
and her of you

in the morning when the mist
rubs with the sun

Spent a day in talk

Spent a day in talk
and a day turning the earth
two actions
one consequence

dream of that courtyard
pillars, the dry dust
on the road
sitting the whole day
placed

but how to achieve it here
hustled by small goals
in their anger
and mine
and partake?

i will not believe all this is
is endurance
there was joy in the recognition
and learning to care
is the other thing

turn to your friend and embrace her
pull the long roots of aggression
make a good soup of the nettle.

for the dreams

for the dreams
invented in the mind
are spurs

a group a gathering of women
with purpose
lives so large we
can
see the power
of a hundred small acts

but so small
bodies like lilliputians
amongst giants

i have seen ants moving
about their common business
shift equivalent mountains
without thought

to think to care to act
to move sideways without fear
and call back the giants
who would have us run with them
into the holocaust.

Knot garden

You have placed here several benches
For the unravelling of thought

The Pool Keeper 1935

across one summer, in an outside pool
built by public conscription, 1860,
he teaches us to swim

his house is cool; shadows have moved inside
like liquid, rippling
his arms are corded like

the rope he pulls us with
his webbing belt broad
around our narrow chests

our luminous and thin ribbed skin.

Walking the ford

minnows dart in shallow clarity
shoals have the habit of birds far off
on the ridge of an escarpment

reeds shoot vertical
offset by wind
wild iris walks to the edge

encased in stones the larval caddis fly
lies low
upstream the great weir gate
sweats against the wide swing of water
the great curve that's always leaving

we are still
watching the ford
preparing. The water is cold
the shift of gravel underfoot
uncertain.

Four different kinds of water

I

her spotted under-wing at rest
Adonis Blue   on Horseshoe Vetch
cropped downs
the cupped sea held
far off
cumulus gathers
over the low weald

II

against chalk cliffs
the parallel lines of flint
the names incised with dates
scored lacerations
blurred by rain
by spray

III

they dive, they jump
from the sea wall
ridged metal would break them
they lick the salt from their skin
throw their trainers high
in the air   laugh as they fall

IV

sea accepts
her skin is more or less water
finds the creases under breasts
the folds her belly makes against her legs
her inner crevices
accept ingress

A Bigger Splash

the diver, when he surfaces, will see
the rocking of an ocean
uncapped waves
and haloed, bright,
an undertow
of shadows
in blue light

a white cliff

a white cliff
hanging without reference
to line
alone

sea submerged by
light as if
no mark
measured the weight
of water

on the lee of the hill
bushes coming to white bloom

Deniz aged five

Deniz is named for the sea
not often calm
sun dips in her hands and flashes
the bright drops fly in the wind

i have seen her in storm
toss at the cliffs
and withdraw
not beaten

restless, restless
lying in the curve
of the earth

NB. Deniz is Turkish word for 'sea'.

That home is not a place . . .

That home is not a place but
a state of mind
is hard to remember

O'Gara street is where I was born,
a little to the left the park runs
down to the river
my friends gather in the evenings
and we walk together over the marshes
brothers and sisters

Living alone
company is less
to carp at
conversations intricately
sidling up to the point
with obvious humour

To begin with there were
houses on the other side
so you couldn't see the marshes
or the trains running like
snakes in the night a glitter with
light from one side to the other,
the youths with their bikes
on the rough ground
blue bottles in the distance
the noise humming and changing in the warm air

We talk of taking those things home
that make home
the act
of choice

makes it a place to be aimed for
with warmth
moss from a damp wood, yellow tormentil
chalk shining in the broad light
of wind, taken up
drawing the mind to its den
of silence.

But she does cry . . .

'But she does cry. How long does not matter, for it is
      doing her good.'
so ends the play
a stage direction to the wind
pages blown over the marshes
one might say voices in the reeds took up the tale
but they did not
what they say tells
other stories less well
trains on the embankment pass over the marshes
they too make easy statements, this way and that
but wind in the dry reeds
sends the dark brown seed heads moving
against each other

to be truthful and honest, as the saying goes, it's impossible
the whole story – late walking, a good lunch, a walk over
      the marshes
with a friend, wading over giving ground, conversation,
clouds moving over dogs and children and the boat
      passing under
the bridge on the way back – is impossible, less than a
      fraction
of what really happens

in the seed heads moving
and moving
against each other

(The first line of this poem is taken from a fragment of a
book of plays on the Kings & Queens of England found on
Hackney Marshes — Autumn 1981.)

Parallax

Always the same walk
across fields
dipping down to a river
where distance blurs the sharp edges
of colour

Middle distant the smooth movement of trees
one trunk slips past another's
sharp grey lines
but that's not it

The rough earth makes uneven shift
smooth parallax is jarred
it is not possible to be with the eyes only
the body also makes its demands
on the mind
come back to the tussocks of strong grass
the bare patches   the indented flint
the uneven print where in the summer gone
a cow made water and stood in it

In my father's store room

I have turned the grindstone
with the wooden handle
till the rough grey stone is a blur
and pushed iron against it

the angle that quiets the
judder and chatter as
fine as a hair
sparks arc across, orange,
there
not there

I have seen a fox flash,
likewise,
to the door of the store room,
eyeing the jumble of tools,
lawnmowers, broken toys,
crockery, frayed rope
coiled on a bent nail,
and boxes of apples
wrapped in autumn
newsprint, greasy
and aromatic

Crumble

I've cut out all the rot
the scab, the canker,

the codling moths
are flown

spot, pox, and worm
excised

my careful knife
has peeled decay

and autumn lies in shreds
about the table.

Felling the apple tree

The fire will not last long; but the wood smoke,
More than the heat will remind us
Of the senders and all that we owe
To the slow labour of sawing
                    Michael Hamburger *from "from a diary"*

We've no regret. Lichen has covered the branches;
this year the apples fell before they ripened.
Sick at heart, the heartwood will burn well,
the fire will warm us; but the wood smoke

will sweeten our breath and the clothes we stand in,
these old clothes, worn like wood, familiar
as this garden. We wear our past in layers,
slowly made, setting with each season.

Nettles have ringed this tree. We scythed mid summer
and still cart sheaves away, to get at the trunk,
to dig for the tap root, knowing this
of the ancestors and all that we owe

to their silence. Pulled with rope, felled by degree,
as we are, father/daughter, as this time
approaches – we will move awkwardly
to the slow labour of sawing.

Yellow plums

as flint lies on chalk
out of the dry august hedgerow
small delicious plums

no bigger than quails eggs
I will pick you a hatful
their hidden stones

load dark leaves
down   the pure
line of hill is in them

jostled there   rubbing
grey bloom from
the far horizon

Windfall

you bring us apples in a plastic bag
they are not smooth and red

they have the summer
painted on their skin

the dents and blemishes
the hidden worms

the wasp holes and the bruise
from summer storms

you bring us Eden
in a plastic bag

a grey Victorian waiting room

a grey Victorian waiting room
between platforms

scuffed lino, the wainscot paint
chipped and scored

with angular graffiti
cursive script

on the back of an old envelope
propped slantwise against skirting board

three words
in pencil

about lost time

Of dew ponds and cattleways (1907)

some water condenses without fail
the grass collects
significant amounts of dew

warm earth and radiance   still air
a swan's down underlay
and flax cotton silk paper straw

one wandering gang of men
hollows the earth
buries such profit under puddled clay

Covert

nestling between
two brassy consonants

and hiding under cover
unconcealed

your o could be a cipher
or lament

a lost breath lying underneath
the ocean

the breathless song of whales
is not more pure

for travelling through storms
so when you leave

embrace me with a calculating heart
and tell me it is over

Notes:

Cinnabar (p. 12)

Heel Schoon – perfect weather
Veranderlyk – changeable, or variable
Bestendig – settled
(Weather indications from the barometric scale, taken from a Dutch barometer.)

In the house of the terracotta warriors (p. 39)

Emperor Qin Shi Huang, the first Emperor of all China, ordered a Mausoleum to be constructed. Many thousands of life-size terracotta figures of warriors were arranged in battle formations there. Previous rulers had entombed slaves and concubines to accompany them in their after life.

Printed in the United Kingdom
by Lightning Source UK Ltd.
130769UK00001B/187-201/A